STEAM in SCOTLAND-1

W.J.V. Anderson & Derek Cross

LONDON

IAN ALLAN LTD

First published 1968
Reprinted 1983

ISBN 0 7110 0359 9

Published by Ian Allan Ltd, Shepperton, Surrey;
and printed by Ian Allan Printing Ltd at their works
at Coombelands in Runnymede, England

To all those who drove, fired, signalled, repaired, and, less
seriously, to all those without whose constant opposition
this would never have been possible.

Acknowledgements

The Publishers wish to acknowledge their thanks to Messrs. S. C.
Crook; J. A. N. Emslie; J. R. P. Hunt; I. Krause; B. Stephenson
and S. E. Teasdale for contributing photographs towards this Album.

The greater part of this volume is the work of W. J. V. Anderson and
D. Cross, who took considerable pains to provide the best from their
photographic collections.

A special vote of thanks is offered to Ruth Gilmour for her part in
typing captions.

Cover: 'Jubilee' class 4-6-0 No 45588 *Kashmir* crosses the Big
Fleet viaduct near Gatehouse of Fleet station with an SLS
Special from Carlisle to Stranraer including the Whithorn
branch on 15 April 1963. *Derek Cross*

Introduction

The dozing traveller on the journey north in a night train from Euston up the West Coast to Scotland felt almost remote from the country he travelled through. From time to time the accents of the various station announcers would break into his sleepy head. There were the Midland accents of Rugby, Stafford and Crewe, the Northern accent of Preston and Lancaster, and the refinement with which "Carlisle Station, Carlisle" was always announced. Suddenly bursting through the window with the early light of a summer's dawn would come a broad Scots tongue as the platform staff at Beattock greeted each other. There now could be no doubt about it — like some promised Mecca the traveller had at last arrived in Scotland. A thrill of excitement would run down the spine of the returning exile; in double measure for the railway enthusiast as the banking engine nudged on to the rear of the train. The train engine would hoot the starting code and, before the answering hoots from the banking engine had died from the surrounding hills, both engines would be roaring their way out of the Station on the five mile climb up Beattock Bank.

Scotland had much to offer the railway enthusiast. The steel web meandered through an incomparable variety of scenery, from the iron foundries of Lanarkshire and the coal mines of Fife, to the remote quiet of the northern highlands. They became part of the country, and added another dimension to the scenery. This must have been especially so in the days prior to the second world war when the locomotives were still beautifully turned out in attractive colours. Now we can only imagine the blue engines of the Caledonian clinging to the very hillside as they climbed up Glenogle, or a beautiful apple green L.N.E.R. A-3 Pacific struggling round the endless curves from Hawick to Shankend, scattering the sheep from the line-side, and filling the air with the uneven beat of its exhaust.

All the best pictures only exist in our imagination, and they will always be better than the pictures we managed to take. This album is devoted to the years between 1945 and the end of steam in Scotland. Looking back on it, this was probably as interesting a period as any to record with a camera. There was much change which brought a big variety of engines to our Scottish metals and, even if the standards of cleanliness deteriorated rapidly, there were shining examples which reminded the younger enthusiasts of what things must have been like before the war. Foremost amongst these was the beautiful condition in which the Haymarket Pacifics were usually kept.

Scotland was also particularly fortunate during this period in that the management of British Railways, Scottish Region, celebrated the final years of steam by rescuing no less than four old engines from museums, restoring them in beautiful array, and running them on many special occasions. By recalling the glories of the past in this manner, a considerable amount of interest in our Railways was re-awakened amongst the general public. There is no doubt that this must have had some commercial impact, though one can be sure the cost accountants would deny this. These engines always ran with full trains, and attracted a great deal of attention from the line-side. What beautiful pictures they made steaming through our delightful countryside; all this at a time when colour film had reached a reasonable state of technical perfection.

As we present this album, we can only think how much better it might have been. There was so much ground to cover that many parts were horribly neglected. Glasgow and its environs alone must have contained literally thousands of good pictures with industrial backgrounds. We regret that we did not have time to cover this area.

It could also be said that there is a certain lack of spontaneity about this collection of pictures. For my own part this was because I was obsessed with the idea of recording the train as part of the scenery, and have therefore missed the elements of human interest which abound on a railway. It is too late now to rectify this, but the country scenery in Scotland is such that it seemed out of place to take pictures on sheds and in city stations.

It is very hard to put one's finger on what was the attraction of train photography. It obviously wasn't just the trains themselves; there were other things, too. The interesting out-of-the-way places we visited, the open air and the ever inconstant weather, the thrill of the chase, the unexpected good luck — all these were elements which, rolled into one, made a fascinating hobby. But perhaps most interesting of all was the people we met. The ganger on his remote stretch in the West Highlands, or the signalman in a lonely cabin; many an interesting conversation on a wide variety of topics helped to pass a quiet spell.

Like so many other things, the giants of steam have gone for ever. A few will sleep out the years in museums. We hope future generations will see them for what they really are — graceful works of mechanical art. They will admire the workmanship, and wonder at the skill of the men who built and drove them, but they will not see the smoke and steam as the wheels roll along the endless ribbon of steel through town and country. I hope we have managed to catch something of this, one of the finest sights created by man. Much is missing, but, to the reader who would wish to sample a fuller flavour, it is still not too late to visit the places where these pictures were taken. Some lines are closed; on others it may just be Diesels that growl their way along, but you may be sure that the rooks still caw in the woods of Dunblane; in spring the cherry blossom clothes the hillsides round Craigellachie, and the young larches yet fill the air with an unforgettable perfume on a dewy morning at Greskine.

W. J. V. Anderson
May 1968.

Section 1 Via Beattock

Left: Stanier Pacific No. 46224 ''Princess Alexandra'' passing Carstairs in Lanarkshire on the up Royal Scot on a March morning in the late 1950s. This was the last member of the class running with a sloping top to the smokebox, a relic of her original streamlined condition. W.J.V.A.

Right: A Horwich-built ''Crab'' 2–6–0 No. 42802 from Grangemouth Depot climbs Beattock Bank on a windy day in May 1958. W.J.V.A.

Right: The Clyde Valley again. Class 5 No. 44719 crosses the Clyde immediately north of Crawford with a Kingmoor – Glasgow goods on the 9th September 1961.   D.C.

Left: Immediately south of Strawfrank Junction (Carstairs), the main line crosses the river on this imposing girder bridge near the tiny village of Pettinain that gave its name to the water troughs and signal box (now closed) at the south end of this bridge. On the 8th June 1963, Class 5 No. 45173 crosses the Clyde with a Motherwell – Kingmoor goods.   D.C.

Right: Beattock from the back! Standard Class 4 MTT No. 80002 banks a Class 5 over the Harthope viaduct on the last stage of the climb to Beattock Summit. Beattock in its day has seen many bankers, ranging in the last fifteen years from the Caley Pacific tanks through Fowler and L.M.S. type 2–6–4T's to these standard engines, the last of the generation of steam bankers.
          D.C.

At Grips with Beattock

Left: On a summer morning 1960, a 3-cylindered rebuilt "Patriot" class 4–6–0 No. 45526 "Morecambe and Heysham" climbs Beattock Bank near Greskine with a London to Glasgow sleeping car express. The train is a very heavy one, probably some 16 vehicles between the 4–6–0 and the banking 2–6–4T. W.J.V.A.

Right: Stanier Class 5 4–6–0 and an unidentified Princess Royal Pacific leave a trail of smoke rolling round the hills as they toil up Beattock Bank on the down Birmingham "Scotsman". July 1954. W.J.V.A.

Above: Elvanfoot – Carstairs Goods hauled by ex-Caledonian 3.F No. 57630 beside the Clyde near Wandel Mill on 15th June 1963.   D.C.

Right: Beattock Summit. Crab 42880 waits in the up refuge siding in August 1961 with a lengthy South-bound fitted freight. A Fairburn 2–6–4 Tank waits on the down main line after banking a North-bound express, ready to cross over and drop back light to Beattock.   D.C.

Left: The neat little Stanier 2–6–2 Tanks that worked in Scotland were few in number but they cropped up in all sorts of places from Glasgow to rural Ayrshire. For several years three were based at Dumfries for the Kirkcudbright and Lockerbie branches, but by the middle of 1961 two had gone to Muirkirk for trains on the steeply graded branch from there to Lanark. In this photo No. 40151 tackles the stiff climb out of Inches with the 9.55 a.m. from Muirkirk to Carstairs in October 1961 shortly before withdrawal.
D.C.

Right top: Throughout the latter part of 1963 and most of 1964, Train 6563 Kingmoor – Edinburgh (Dalry Road) Goods was worked most afternoons by an ex-L.N.E.R. engine as the last leg of a diagram embracing Edinburgh – Newcastle – Carlisle, and back to Edinburgh over the erstwhile Caledonian main line. The normal power being a B.1, though a V.2 was sometimes used. This photo taken in June 1964 shows B.1 No. 61029 "Chamois" shortly after rounding the Carstairs avoiding line from Strawfrank Junction and starting the climb to Cobbinshaw Summit. The train is approaching Carnwath Station, and the imposing building in the background is not some Laird's residence but Scotland's top security Borstal!
D.C.

Right: Rebuilt Scot No. 46165 "The Ranger" (12th London Regiment) passes Greskine with a North-bound summer Saturday special S37; those with access to the code will be able to identify this train.
W.J.V.A.

Pacifics on Beattock

Left: A North-bound sleeping car train climbs Beattock Bank early on a beautiful July morning in 1959. The train engine is the "Penultimate Duchess" No. 46256, named after the designer Sir William A. Stanier, F.R.S. Resplendent in a new coat of maroon paint, she differs from her sisters in that she is equipped with roller bearings and electric light. Furthermore, the cab side sheets do not go down so far.
W.J.V.A.

Centre: Following hard on the heels of No. 46256, another Pacific, No. 46223 "Princess Alice", also climbs the bank near Greskine on a sleeping car express.
W.J.V.A.

Right: The 10.5 a.m. Glasgow Central to Birmingham train in May 1957, between Abingdon and Crawford in the Upper Clyde Valley. Princess Royal Pacific No. 46211 "Queen Maud".
W.J.V.A.

Left: "Jubilee" class 3-cylindered 4–6–0 No. 45738 "Samson" needs all her strength to lift this fourteen coach North-bound train up Beattock Bank early one morning in 1963. Much-needed Banking assistance is provided by a B.R. Standard 2–6–4T.   W.J.V.A.

Right: One of Britain's Titled trains whose name never appeared in any time-table. As a matter of interest the train never appeared in any public time-table either, for this is the mid-day shopping train from Beattock to Beattock Summit, known all over the old Caley main line as "The Siege". These trains, of which two ran each way on Saturdays, were run for the benefit of the wives and families living in the railway cottages on Beattock Bank and at the Summit to get down to Moffat for their weekend's shopping. Another interesting feature of the working was that while it was always one engine (out of Beattock's stud of bankers) and one coach going up the hill; on the returning working, any bank engines that were waiting at the Summit to return to Beattock Station were attached to the coach as well as its own engine, so it has been known for the South-bound Siege to have three engines on its one coach. On this occasion, the 1st June 1964, the North-bound morning Siege hauled by Fairburn 2–6–4T No. 42214, is passing through one of the rock cuttings at Harthope seven-eighths of the way up the hill.   D.C.

Below: On a rather sombre day in September 1955, the sun found a window in the sky just as Pacific No. 46230 "Duchess of Buccleuch" passed Harthope on the ascent to Beattock Summit with the 10.10 a.m London to Glasgow express.   W.J.V.A

Right: In July 1954, the Down "Royal Scot" climbs Beattock Bank near Harthope. The engine is one of the later Stanier Pacifics No. 46255 "City of Hereford". This picture was only possible for a few months; the railway telephone wires have just been buried for a short section to make a safe passage for even more unsightly high tension wires which have yet to be erected.
W.J.V.A.

Opposite left: A mile short of Beattock Summit not long after dawn on a fine summer morning in 1962, Pacific No. 46237 "City of Bristol" fills the still air with the unmistakable heavy hollow beat of a Duchess. The train is a North-bound overnight extra from London to Glasgow.
W.J.V.A.

Opposite right: In July 1961, rebuilt Scot 4–6–0 No. 46105 "Cameron Highlander" climbs Beattock with a Manchester to Glasgow Express.
W.J.V.A.

Right: The unrebuilt Patriot class 4–6–0's, designed by Fowler for the L.M.S., were rarely seen in Scotland. In this picture one of them, No. 45549, is piloting a rebuilt Scot 4–6–0 No. 46102 on a heavy Manchester to Glasgow train. The location is again Harthope, April 1957.
W.J.V.A.

Left: Lamington, in May 1964. Duchess No. 46244 "King George VI" heads for Glasgow with the 9.0 a.m. from Carlisle. The use of a Duchess on this train, even at the end of their career at Kingmoor, was rare, as the load was normally considered to be within a Britannia's capabilities . . . on this occasion one of the latter must have failed on shed.   D.C.

Right: One of the many summer Saturday extras toils up Beattock Bank in July 1958. The pilot is Class 2P 4–4–0 No. 40695. The train engine with steam sanding hard on and probably doing most of the work is Stanier Jubilee Class 4–6–0 No. 45702 "Colossus". Out of sight round the corner a third engine – one of the Beattock bankers, a Stanier 2–6–4T – is giving the whole cavalcade a shove.   W.J.V.A.

Below: The standard Class 3MT 2–6–0's were a rare breed and throughout their brief careers were very localised in distribution. In Scotland they had two limited spheres of influence, round Kilmarnock and round Motherwell. For a short spell in 1961 one of the latter appeared fairly regularly on a freight over the Clyde Valley main line. No. 77005 heads north beside the Clyde in September 1961.   D.C.

Left: Carstairs Junction. This photograph, taken on the 15th May 1964, shows a Perth – Carlisle parcels train leaving the yard behind Stanier Class 5 No. 44921.   D.C.

Left below: An up freight coasts downhill into Beattock Station. The engine is a Horwich 2–6–0 No. 42735. The line curving to the right is the branch to Moffat.   W.J.V.A.

Right: Thunder clouds pile up over the hills as Duchess Pacific No. 46245 ''City-of-London'' rushes through Beattock Station on the down ''Mid-day Scot'' in August 1961. Two down freight trains wait in the loops for their turns to tackle Beattock Bank behind Stanier Class 5's Nos. 44793 and 45122 respectively.   W.J.V.A.

Below: With a nice clean chimney, which does not entirely please the photographer, Stanier Princess Royal Pacific No. 46209 ''Princess Beatrice'' tackles Beattock Bank with the down Birmingham Scotsman. The only smoke in evidence is coming from the banking 2–6–4T.   W.J.V.A.

Below right: Standard 4 No. 76090 of Beattock leaves the lonely station of Elvanfoot with a South-bound crane train on 4th July 1964.   D.C.

Left: "Positively the Last Appearance" . . . well, anyhow, positively the last of several Last Appearances. Ex-GNSR 4–4–0 No. 49 "Gordon Highlander" coasts into Carstairs under the graceful signal gantry at the north end of the station with a Branch Line Excursion. The train was en route from Douglas Water colliery (the end of the old Lanark/Muirkirk line at present) to Edinburgh. This in actual fact was No. 49's last run on a special train and was on 16th October 1965.
D.C.

Right: In days of steam, locomotive failures out on the road were comparatively rare. In July 1954, Pacific No. 46230 "Duchess of Buccleuch" ran hot while working the "up" "Royal Scot" through the upper Clyde Valley. She had to come off the train at Abington; you might suppose that in such an outlandish spot help would be a long time in coming. With considerable ingenuity and alacrity a "Caley" Jumbo 0–6–0 was purloined off a down pick-up goods, and one of the 2–6–4T Beattock bankers was hastily summoned from the Summit box some ten miles to the South. The "Scot" was on its way again a mere 45 minutes late. In this picture 46230 cools off in a siding at Abington while Jubilee Class 4–6–0 No. 45731 "Perseverance" passes on a Glasgow to Manchester express. W.J.V.A.

Below: Carstairs again. Jubilee Class 4–6–0 No. 45705 "Seahorse" leaving Carstairs for Glasgow on 15th May 1964, with the second portion of the morning Liverpool and Manchester – Glasgow express.
D.C.

Smoke and Freight

Right: As soon as Horwich Crab 2–6–0 No. 42793 passes Greskine distant signal at caution, the driver shuts off steam. The other driver in the Banking 2–6–4T will keep some steam on until the train stops at the home signal; though both drivers hope the home will have cleared by the time they get there, not that this light North-bound train would have been difficult to restart.

W.J.V.A.

Far right: Ministry of Supply "Austerity" 2–10–0 No. 90750 seems to be making an unnecessary amount of smoke as she works a South-bound freight over favourable grades north of Lockerbie, in Dumfriesshire.

W.J.V.A.

Left: Ex-Caledonian Railway 0–4–4T No. 55237 on the Moffat Push and Pull train.

J. A. N. Emslie.

Below left: With the River Clyde behind, Stanier Pacific No. 46230 "Duchess of Buccleuch" accelerates the Up "Royal Scot" away from a P.W. Slack between Abingdon and Crawford in May 1957. W.J.V.A.

Below right: In March 1958, Stanier Pacific No. 46256 "Sir William A. Stanier F.R.S." passes South through Crawford in Lanarkshire with a recently introduced Anglo Scottish flyer, "The Caledonian". W.J.V.A.

Left: A2 Pacific No. 60535 about to leave Carstairs on a Glasgow express in July 1964.
J. R. P. Hunt.

Right: In July 1954, ex-Caledonian Jumbo 0–6–0 No. 57414 climbs Beattock with a weed-killing train. Two of the tenders being used as tanks are of L.N.W.R. pattern. The third is unmistakably the tender off an ex-Highland railway Clan Goods 4–6–0.
W.J.V.A.

Section 2 Ayrshire Scenes

The end of steam in Ayrshire. On Saturday, 1st October 1966, Class 5 No. 45423 looks forlornly out of Ayr shed, her last job done. On the Monday the diesels took over and by the following Friday 45423, along with the bulk of Ayr's steam locos, was towed away for scrap. D.C.

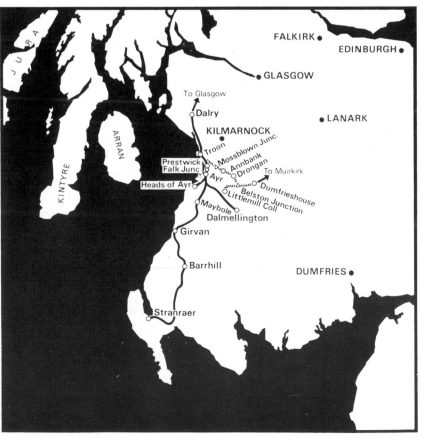

For some years after the war Ayr boasted two or three Austerity 2–8–0's for working some of their heavier Coal Trains. By the early 1960s their two remaining engines of this Class were confined almost entirely to the difficult turns to and from Waterside. Apart from their strength on the hills, their brakes were good enough to pass even the critical opinion of the Ayr Drivers. Their transfer to the East Coast in the summer of 1963 was a great loss. On the 1st March 1963, at the end of the bitter winter of that year, No. 90319 crosses the River Ayr at the east end of Ayr station with K.36, an empty wagon train to Waterside. An unusual feature this day was the ''wrong line'' working through Ayr Station, owing to the late arrival of the mail train from the south blocking the down platform while it was un-loaded.   D.C.

By the last year of the 1950s, Ayr and the Somerset and Dorset were the last two areas that were still using the Fowler 2.P's. While the S & D Locos were used day in and day out on local services, Ayr's were used only on minor jobs to and from Kilmarnock, and the odd relief train to Glasgow. On the occasion of the Ayr Spring Holiday in April 1961, 2.P No. 40595 leaves Ayr with one such relief to Glasgow, probably the last occasion when a 2.P worked an Ayr – Glasgow passenger train.   D.C.

For some years after the war, Ayr's passenger pilot was this 0–4–4T No. 55262. This engine, despite her being of hated Caledonian origin in the stronghold of the G. & S.W., was kept in immaculate condition right up till 1959, when the arrival of the D.M.U.'s rendered her job and her days at an end. In July 1958, 55262 draws a rake of empty coaches out of Ayr's No. 2 platform.   D.C.

Below: During the late winter of 1966, N.C.B. No. 18, a six-coupled Barclay and the "Black sheep" of Waterside, was on loan to the Glenburn Colliery to deal with extra production. On Saturday March 19th she ran back light from Glenburn (Prestwick) to her depot at Waterside. For this journey she had two complete crews, one B.R. and one N.C.B., and this gave rise to a hilarious episode in Ayr. It was decided that she take water at the column at the south end of Ayr station and this was duly done. While watering was in progress, the B.R. driver expressed himself of the opinion that the boiler wouldn't boil an egg. This produced some dirty looks from the N.C.B. crew and remarks about the quality of the coal, which was mostly slack and very dusty at that. As it was blowing the usual gale up the Doon Valley it was decided to water the coal in the bunker, so with a lot of manoeuvring and advice from all sides the bunker was positioned alongside the water column and the bag dropped in . . . Big Brother B.R. then turned the water column on and within seconds there was a mass exodus of three very dirty and wet figures from the footplate; alas the firehole door was level with the floor and the torrent of water coming from the bunker flowed straight into the fire. A large amount of steam was generated and also a large amount of temper from the N.C.B. men . . . made worse by the driver (B.R.) who was laughing so much that he couldn't turn the water off.   D.C.

Right: The Mighty McCann, the Stirling Moss of Stranraer, makes the welkin ring as Class 5 No. 45168 accelerates southwards out of Ayr with a Falkland Junction to Stranraer goods on 1st April 1966.   D.C.

Right: "The Twins", the name by which the Littlemill colliery train was known. This photo, taken in May 1961, shows a rare crossing at Belston Junction. "The Twins", running late, are propelling their train off the branch to Littlemill back on to the old A & C line to Ayr. In a refuge loop is Crab No. 42805 with the midday Ayr – Littlemill empties, which theoretically should have made the crossing at Drongan. The engines on "The Twins" are Caley 3.F 0–6–0's Nos. 57644 & 57569. D.C.

Left: "Where are ye gang next, Mr. Cross?" To my answer of Tarbolton old station, the driver of this S.L.S. Special in June 1962 went on "Ye'll be wantin some smoke there then." "Yes", I answered hopefully, not for a moment anticipating what was to come. Fairburn L.M.S.-built 2–6–4T No. 42196 darkens the sky and obliterates the closed station of Tarbolton, between Annbank and Mauchline, as she tops the 1 in 70 with the Stephenson Loco Society's tour of the Ayrshire Branches. D.C.

Right: For some strange reason the Fowler 4.F's were rare specimens in Scotland, just as their successors the Stanier 8.F's have been. In the early part of this decade Kilmarnock had two and Ayr the same number, of which 44189, seen here at Annbank with a Whitehill – Ayr Harbour coal train on 20th October 1962, was one. This Whitehill job was a terror, as the branch into the mine left the now closed Cumnock A & C line at Dykes Junction and made its way up to Whitehill mine by means of a short reversing loop with very steep grades. Like a similar arrangement at Polquhairn mine the stops of the reversing line overhung a deep gully, and it was into this gully that 44189 made her last trip some months after this photo was taken. D.C.

Left: Annbank Junction on the 25th August 1961, with Caley 0–6–0's 57569 and 57633 coming off the branch from Drongan with "The Twins" from Littlemill Colliery. This was among the last workings of "The Twins", as soon after this a bridge strengthening on the Rankiston Branch and a reorganisation of the Ayrshire coal trains enabled this train to be worked by one Crab. The amusement of the engine crews was due to the discomfort of the photographer, perched like some overfed vulture up a rather rickety signal which was replaced soon after!
D.C.

Below: During their short period in Ayr, the B.1.s worked mainly to and from the Central Ayrshire Coal Field over the lines from Ayr to Annbank, Drongan, and Mauchline. On this March morning towards the end of the bitter winter of 1963, B.1. No. 61355 slows for a signal stop at Mossblown Junction, between Ayr and Annbank, with a rake of empty wagons that had been stored at Annbank and were being pressed into service to handle the increased output from the local collieries. Mossblown Junction, like the branch it controlled to and from Auchencruive 4 and 5 Collieries, has since ceased to exist. D.C.

Top: The closed station of Drongan and its attendant loops was the Crewe of the Central Ayrshire coal fields. It was the only passing loop between Annbank and the mines round Rankiston and Cumnock, and it is now even more important as the junction to Scotland's newest colliery at Killoch served by a line constructed as late as 1960. Taking this new line to Killoch in this photo on the 16th April 1965 is A.37 Ayr Harbour – Killoch empties, hauled by Standard Class 4 MT No. 76096; while Crab No. 42740 coasts down the hill and into one of Drongan's loops with A.29 coal train from Littlemill Mine.　　D.C.

Centre: Until the "Paddy" (Stranraer – Euston Boat Train) was diverted from the direct line to Dumfries and re-routed through Ayr, the line from Ayr to Mauchline was normally only used for goods traffic. The exceptions to this were certain excursions run from the south to Ayr or Largs during the summer months. The late evening of the 1st June 1962 finds one such excursion, returning from Ayr to Carlisle, tackling the long climb from Blackhouse Junction to Tarbolton on the approaches to Mossblown, hauled by Clan Pacific No. 72009 "Clan Stewart".　　D.C.

Bottom: Two strangers in Ayrshire meet at Mossblown Junction. B.1 No. 61243 climbs towards the Ayrshire Plateau with a load of slurry from Whitehill mine for the Coal Board's Electricity generating station at Barony Colliery, near Auchinleck. This train was always a headache to work, as it had to be worked from Annbank up to Mauchline over several miles at 1 in 70, and the B.1's were not the answer . . . in fact this particular train stalled beyond Annbank. The other stranger was Standard Class 4 No. 76096, only recently shedded at Ayr. This train has a load of coal from Barony Colliery to Ayr.　　D.C.

The Dalmellington Branch

Below left: From 1960 onwards, apart from one job on a Saturday afternoon, the passenger services up the Doon Valley became dieselised. This Saturday train leaving Ayr about noon, came from Kilmarnock, and to the end of passenger working on the branch was always steam worked. On a sunny Saturday in April 1961, Fairburn 2–6–4 Tank No. 42190 restarts this train from the rustic station of Hollybush.   D.C.

Below right: On the 4th April 1964, Standard Class 3 2–6–0 No. 77016 of Hurlford heading for Ayr, and ultimately Kilmarnock, with the Saturday midday train from Dalmellington. This was the last day of passenger services on the Doon Valley line, a line worked over the last three years of its life by diesel rail buses with the one exception of the extra Saturday lunch-time trains, the last of which is shown.   D.C.

Right: The old G. & S.W. was built on coal and this is still true today; aided albeit by commuters trying to get away from the nastiness that coal and resultant wealth has created. To get the coal to the G. & S.W. railheads the various Mining Coys., and latterly the N.C.B., maintained a stock of their own locos. In May 1961, the yards at Waterside show both B.R. and N.C.B. locos side by side. N.C.B. 0–4–0 Barclay Tank, West Ayr Area No. 19, draws a load of coal from the washer while "Crab" No. 42801 passes with a short freight from Dalmellington, a freight that will be made up with coal from Waterside for Ayr Harbour.   D.C.

Right: On 8th April 1965, 2–6–0 No. 42917 takes some 55 empty wagons from Ayr up the Dalmellington branch to the Waterside complex of coal mines. This impressive viaduct is between Dalrymple Junction and Hollybush. W.J.V.A.

Opposite: On a summer's day in 1958, 2.P No. 40590 coasts down across the graceful Dalrymple Viaduct with the midday train from Dalmellington to Ayr and Kilmarnock. D.C.

Ayr – Girvan and the Heads of Ayr Branch

Left: The cry of "Nae Brakes" that greeted every new engine to come to Ayr did not apply to the B.1s for passenger work, much as they were distrusted on un-fitted freights; and throughout the summer of 1963 one of Ayr's six of these locos, No. 61261, was kept in superb condition as main line pilot and for working passenger trains to and from Butlins Camp at Heads of Ayr. On 18th June 1963, she pilots Class 5 No. 44808 on a school excursion from Ibrox (Glasgow) to Girvan on the 1 in 70 up to Dalrymple Junction, through a rainstorm that was ferocious even by Ayrshire standards.   D.C.

Below left: Snow again. In dealing with some of my shots at Girvan and Maybole, I mentioned the great blizzard of 3rd March 1965, and its disastrous effects on D.M.U's, even after the Stranraer line was ploughed out. Late on the evening of the 4th the line from Ayr to Girvan was opened for traffic, for it was not till the following day that it was opened throughout to Stranraer. On March 5th, a service of trains was worked to Girvan in the morning by steam locos and stock, and one of these trains is seen here leaving Maybole Station hauled by Standard Class 4.MT No. 76096, en route from Girvan back to Ayr and connections to Glasgow by DMU.   D.C.

Below right: Class 5 No. 45162, returning from Stranraer on the 4.20 to Glasgow on Saturday, 6th March 1965, approaching Maybole with Kildoor Hill in the background. The engine was working as far as Ayr, where passengers transferred to the normal DMU service for Glasgow.   D.C.

Below: Class 5s, Nos. 44767 & 45168, restart a train of empty car vans off the Girvan Goods branch, 28th June 1966.   D.C.

Top left: In July 1966, the wooded hills of the Girvan Valley between Dailly and Kilkerran form the backdrop for Caprotti Class 5, No. 73145, and "Black" 5, No. 44999, as they head toward Ayr with the 7.55 a.m. Stranraer to Falkland Junction Goods.   D.C.

Top right: One of Ayr's ill-starred B.1's cautiously descending the 1 in 70 from Dalrymple Junction to Ayr with an early morning coal train from Waterside to Ayr Harbour, in March 1964. Because of their reputation for bad brakes these engines were seldom used on the Watersides and, after one ran away and caused a pile up at Ayr No. 2, they were banned altogether. Loco No. 61261 seen here nearing Glengall Junction. D.C.

Bottom left: Another last run, this time for Caley 2.F's Nos. 57355 & 57375, being hauled "dead" from Stranraer to the breaker's yard at Troon Harbour. 57375 figures elsewhere in this album of photos hauling a passenger train on the Whithorn Branch. This photo, on the 20th May 1964, shows the two condemned locos in the Girvan Valley between Dailly and Kilkerran, hauled by Class 5 No. 45126.   D.C.

Bottom right: "Couple the Bargany". This was the cry that used to be heard in Ayr Loco whenever the number of wagons at Bargany Colliery became too great for the afternoon goods to clear. On this April day in 1961, ex-Caley 3.F No. 57596 couples "Crab" No. 42801 with the afternoon Bargany to Ayr Harbour coal train as it climbs the short sharp bank from the Doon Viaduct to Dalrymple Junction.   D.C.

Left: The Bargany coal pit was tucked unexpectedly away in the beautiful Girvan valley on the line from Ayr to Stranraer. Horwich 2–6–0 No. 42917 and Stanier 4–6–0 No. 45161 tackling the steepest part of the climb up to Crosshill summit pass through Dailly Station shortly after leaving the pit. A thin drizzle is making things particularly difficult for the locomotives. April 1965.   W.J.V.A.

Right: The 1st June 1963, finds Ayr's pet B.1 No. 61261 once again on a passenger train. This time the train is the 9.0 a.m. Ayr – Heads of Ayr train (for Butlin's Camp) crossing the River Doon near Alloway on the surviving section of the Ayr – Dunure & Turnberry Light Railway, retained for serving Butlin's Camp on some dozen-and-a-half Saturdays in summer. The engine off the 9.0 a.m. from Ayr subsequently worked the 9.20 Heads of Ayr – Edinburgh through train, and throughout that summer this was one of the B.1's regular jobs.   D.C.

Left: Class 5, No. 45162, tackles the start of the 1 in 54 out of Girvan with the 11.25 Glasgow to Stranraer boat train. 6th March 1965. D.C.

Right: Ex-Caledonian 2.F 0–6–0 No. 57375 at Stranraer Town station, with an S.L.S. Special from Glasgow to Stranraer and Whithorn. D.C.

Below: After a day and night of torrential rain, the midnight goods from Glasgow to Stranraer ran into a landslide at Pinwherry. Here the breakdown train, work completed, heads back to Hurlferd hauled by 4.F No. 44281 with the re-railed wagons. 12th September 1962. D.C.

'Sou-West' Viaducts

Below: One rather startling exception to the graceful stone viaducts that were so much a feature of the old G. & S.W. was the viaduct across the Ligg Burn, between Pinwherry and Barrhill, on the Stranraer Line. On a bitter morning, the 28th February 1963, a Class 5 crosses the Ligg Viaduct with the 8.10 a.m. Stranraer – Ayr goods. Loco 45485 with a very co-operative Stranraer crew, who, when they saw the photographer having difficulty keeping his feet on a frozen snow drift, stopped and waited for him to get into position before slipping their brakes and coasting down to Pinwherry.   D.C.

Right: The Pinmore Viaduct in high summer of 1965. This viaduct, five miles south of Girvan on the Stranraer Line, must be among the most graceful and photogenic of all the Scottish Viaducts and is once again typical of the G. & S.W. bridges, being built of stone quarried virtually from its base. The central piers have been bound with metal hoops at a later date (possibly during the First War), but even this cannot spoil the grace and symmetry of the structure, thrown into contrast by the dark woods behind. The train is the Saturday afternoon boat express from Stranraer to Newcastle on the 10th of July, hauled by Class 5's 45365 and 45160.　　　D.C.

Right below: At the same location, "Jubilee" No. 45659 "Drake", with an Easter Monday relief train from Stranraer to Glasgow, 1965.　　　D.C.

Left: Class 5's at rest on Stranraer Shed.

Left below: B.R. Class 6 4–6–2 No. 72005 Clan, about to depart from Stranraer.

Right: Two Crabs, Nos. 42863 & 42803 wait in Girvan Platform with a ballast train from Irvine to Stranraer on 22nd June 1966. To get this combination was rare, for though many of the Ayr drivers would far sooner have had a Crab for freight work on the Stranraer road than a Black 5, by the time this picture was taken Ayr's rapidly dwindling stock of Crabs was getting into a deplorable state mechanically. However, on this occasion, despite rain and a strong wind, the two started out of Girvan up the 1 in 54 of Glendoune Bank without a slip, and made good time right to New Luce where the pilot was detached. A fortnight later this ballast ran again, and when I enquired if it was likely to have the two Crabs I was told in no uncertain terms that it certainly was not . . . they couldn't risk these old things breaking down and blocking the Stranraer line. The supreme irony was that the Caprotti Standard 5 and Black 5 that ultimately worked this second train came to a stand at the Waterworks, half-way up the 1 in 54, for twenty minutes while they got their breath back, and this with the same load as the Crabs had taken successfully before.

D.C.

Right: Early on the misty morning of 18th January 1966, a sad and rather pathetic convoy of condemned locomotives passes Falkland Junction (Ayr) en route for Kilmarnock, to collect another condemned engine, and ultimately the scrap yards of a Wishaw Steel Works. "Crab" No. 42740 hauls sister engine 42800, Ivatt Class 2. No. 46413 and Standard Class 4 76112 on their last journey.   D.C.

Right below: Last journeys for a motley selection of six coupled goods engines. Class 5 No. 45126 hauls a rake of condemned locos past Lochgreen Junction and on to the Branch to Troon and the West of Scotland's Ship-breaking yard at Troon Harbour. The first two of these condemned locos, both ex-Caledonian 2.F class 0–6–0's Nos. 57375 & 57355, had been brought from Stranraer, and the last of this sad convoy, an ex-N.B. J.37 class No. 64626 was collected from Ayr on the way past. The short reign of these N.B. freight engines at Ayr ended by their perishing on the rock of all "foreign" freight engines in Ayrshire . . . "Nae brakes".   D.C.

Right: After their displacement from the Ayr/Glasgow services by D.M.U.'s, the 2.P's worked out their remaining days at Ayr on stopping trains to Dalmellington and Kilmarnock. Early in 1960, Rail Buses took over the Dalmellington jobs, leaving the 2.P's with various turns to Kilmarnock. The most important of these was the 5.10 p.m. Ayr/Kilmarnock, that conveyed the Post Office sorting van for connection with the 5.30 ex-St. Enoch to Carlisle, and ultimately the up West Coast Postal. In April 1961, towards the very end of their lengthy reign on the G. & S.W., 2.P. No. 40602 heads the 5.10 p.m. from Ayr through Falkland Junction towards Kilmarnock.   D.C.

Right below: While the Nith Valley line during 1964 was frequently traversed by A.2 Pacifics, and occasionally by the other types of ex-L.N.E.R. 4–6–2's, by the following year these engines were distinctly rare. Whit Saturday, the 5th June 1965, produced one such working, on a relief from Bradford to Glasgow. A.1 No. 60154 "Bon Accord" approaches Dalry Junction, off the Kilmarnock line, on a normal wet Ayrshire afternoon.   D.C.

Left: With an impressive back-drop of cloud, Jubilee class 4–6–0 No. 45711 ''Courageous'' accelerates past the site of Monkton Station, just North of Prestwick. The train is the 4.20 p.m. Stranraer to Glasgow St. Enoch.
W.J.V.A.

Right: An evening local from Ayr to Glasgow passes Monkton in July 1954. The engine is a Class 2.P 4–4–0 No. 40590.
W.J.V.A.

Section 3
Dumfries – Kilmarnock
and the Portpatrick Line

Dumfries

Left: The Scottish region's preserved Pre-Grouping locos were like ageing Prima Donnas, with a whole series of "Last" appearances throughout 1964 and 1965. This photo, taken in October 1965, shows ex-Highland Jones Goods No. 103 at Dumfries coaling plant, on what was her last run with a passenger train, an excursion from Glasgow to Dumfries via the Nith Valley, and back via Lockerbie and the Caledonian line. D.C.

Right: 31st July 1964. Dumfries Station, with the 6.50 a.m. Carlisle to Glasgow postal and parcels train waiting to set out for the North. While the ex-L.N.E.R. A.2 Pacifics were seldom used on passenger working, this heavy and important parcels train was one of their more regular jobs, and the engine shown, No. 60535 "Hornet's Beauty", was one of the most regular performers. D.C.

Left: A post-war development at Dumfries was the construction of a large factory by Messrs. Metalbox Ltd. at Maxwellton, on the Dumfries/Stranraer line some three miles west of Dumfries. It is this factory that has been instrumental in keeping the surviving three miles of this line open as far as Maxwellton. In June 1964, Ivatt Class 2 No. 46450 passes Dumfries with the morning shunt from Metalbox to the yard at the east end of Dumfries, whence it was worked forward to Kingmoor by anything that happened to be handy, and, incidentally, produced some great variety of motive power.   D.C.

Right: Fairburn 2–6–4 Tank Engines Nos. 42196 and 42689 cross at the North end of Dumfries Station on the 1st June 1963. 42196 approaches with an early afternoon stopping train from Kirkcudbright, while her sister engine waits to back on to the end of this train and form another train to Kirkcudbright. The Nith Valley Main Line disappears Northwards behind the back coaches.   D.C.

The Portpatrick and Wigtown Lines

Left top: Ex-Caledonian 2F 0–6–0 No. 57375 works a railway enthusiasts' special on the Whithorn branch; seen here crossing the River Bladnock, a mile south of Wigtown, 14th April 1963. D.C.

Left below: The Stranraer – Dumfries line saw most of its activity during the hours of darkness, and long passenger trains in daylight were rare. A few weeks before the line finally closed, however, the Sunday peace of rural Galloway was rudely shattered by convoys of ten coach troop specials over this line on consecutive Sundays. These trains ran between Stranraer and Woodburn on the North Eastern and were run in connection with Territorial Army training in Northern Ireland. This photo shows train 1X31, returning from Woodburn to Stranraer on the 30th May, crossing the Big Water of Fleet Viaduct near Gatehouse Station behind Engine 72008 "Clan Macleod". D.C.

Below: Among the features of the Whithorn Peninsular is its extraordinary equitable climate. In 1964, Wigtown station could hardly boast its being the busiest in Scotland; it could boast the two biggest Monkey Puzzle trees. These make an unusual background for Standard 2.MT No. 78016, as it sits dreaming in the sunshine with the thrice-weekly goods for Whithorn in July 1964. Two months later the Branch was closed. D.C.

Left: The thrice-weekly Newton Stewart — Whithorn Goods at Millisle in July 1964, shortly before this fascinating rural line closed for good. Standard 2.MT No. 78016 passes the imposing signal box at Millisle, the only signal box on the line.   D.C.

Right: Troop Special on the Dumfries — Stranraer line. Clan No. 72007 "Clan Mackintosh" tackles the climb from the Big Water of Fleet Viaduct to Gatehouse of Fleet Station, with the sinister basalt columns of the Clints of Dromoree in the background. The train was 1X30 Woodburn — Stranraer Troop Special. 30th May 1965.   D.C.

Right below: One of Ivatt's fascinating light Moguls, No. 46467, climbing the short steep bank between Kirkcowan and Whauphill on the Whithorn Branch on the 26th April 1964, with the Wednesday goods train from Newton Stewart to Whithorn. The Whithorn Branch had its operating snags without a doubt, including no less than four sets of level crossing gates that had to be operated by the train crews. It was also subject to occasional flooding but was not greatly worried by grades, with one exception. The station of Whauphill, serving the agricultural hinterland of the Whithorn Peninsular, was nearly 200 ft. above the level of the coastal plain that the railway followed for most of its length. The South Scottish term "whaup" means a curlew, a bird that is not addicted to urban civilisation, and so Whauphill and its approaches were bleak and steep and, of the two, the climb from the north side (shown in this photograph) was the most difficult, especially in the teeth of one of the all too frequent Southerly gales that swept up the Irish Sea and battered themselves against the highlands of the Whithorn.   D.C.

The Nithsdale Line (Dumfries to Kilmarnock)

Left: Early morning in Upper Nithsdale. Class 5 No. 44943 crosses the Crawick Water some ¾ mile north of Sanquhar on a May morning in 1963. The train is a North-bound goods from Kingmoor Yard to Ayr or Kilmarnock. D.C.

Below: The Nith Valley line is peculiar in that the stiffest part of the climbing occurs in the lower part of the valley, a situation more like some of the Welsh lines than Scotland. Between Kirkconnel and New Cumnock the line is nearly level and follows the meandering River Nith through miles of flat water meadows. In April 1964, Standard Class 5 No. 73057 skirts the river near Upper Cairn with a North-bound goods from Carlisle. D.C.

Right top: The year 1964 was hailed in Scottish ornothological circles as the second year the Osprey returned to nest on a small loch near Aviemore. It was also the year when Peppercorn's A.1 Class Pacific 60131 "Osprey" made several appearances in Glasgow on Saturday relief trains from Leeds. The means used to return this loco to Holbeck were many and devious, of which the most common was the 2.0 p.m. Glasgow (St. Enoch) – Carlisle stopping train on a Monday afternoon. On this Monday in June 1964, No. 60131 works the 2.0 p.m. round the curve off the Ballochmyle Viaduct between Mauchline and Brackenhill Junction; a lowly job for such an engine but rather better than the Monday morning paper train from Glasgow to Dumfries, which was one of the other ways of returning the N.E. Pacific . . . the paper train was usually one van only south of Kilmarnock! D.C.

Right below: One of the features of working over the Nith Valley line in 1964 was the extraordinary variety of motive power that appeared on everyday trains. Apart from the surviving L.M.S. Pacifics, both types of Standard Pacific and also all four types of L.N.E. Pacific were regular performers. In this picture, 60522 "Straight Deal" approaches Garrochburn sidings, south of Kilmarnock, with a fitted freight from Kilmarnock to Brent on a July evening in 1964. D.C.

Right: The Nith Valley line rises to a summit at Polquhap between Cumnock and New Cumnock. This summit is approached from the north by the notorious Blackfaulds Cutting that fills with snow on every possible occasion. On this cold April day in 1962, Caley 3.F 0–6–0 emerges from Blackfaulds under the main Kilmarnock/Dumfries road and on to the curving embankment that leads up the last few hundred yards to the summit at Polquhap Farm. Loco No. 57601. D.C.

Below: During the last week of the goods service, Class 5 No. 45497 starts on the ferocious climb out of Catrine in the wooded valley of the River Ayr with the daily goods from Catrine to Ayr. The use of a Class 5 running tender first on this job was unusual, as the normal power at this time was either a Crab or B.1, and this may have been an engine pressed into service after a failure. D.C.

Left: Shortly after their restoration and return to traffic, ex-C.R. 4–2–2 No. 123 and ex-N.B.R. 4–4–0 No. 256 "Glen Douglas" work an excursion from Dumfries to Glasgow near Carronbridge. September 1959.   W.J.V.A.

Below left: The down "Thames Clyde Express", headed by a "Scot" 4–6–0 No. 46108 Seaforth Highlander, rounds one of the very sharp but beautifully super-elevated curves in the Drumlanrig gorge on the Nith Valley route. It is interesting to note that the headboard has not been put on properly. It is sitting proud of the top of the smokebox, causing turbulence, which is drawing the smoke down to obscure the engine driver's view ahead. August 1957.   W.J.V.A.

Below right: In May 1959, Class 2P 4–4–0 No. 40686 hauls the 3.5 p.m. all stations from Dumfries to Glasgow. This location is on the long but picturesque stretch between Carronbridge and Sanquhar. Unlike most of her English sisters, the engine still carries a Midland pattern chimney; in fact, most of the Scottish-based engines of this class did; a sign of St. Rollox individuality?   W.J.V.A.

Left: Ex-North British Railway 4–4–2T No. 67454 forlornly awaits the end in the scrap yard at Kilmarnock Works.

Below: Brackenhill Junction, on the Nith Valley main line between Mauchline and Auchinleck, was the junction for the Catrine Branch which dropped steeply for 1½ miles from the main line to the little textile town of Catrine in the valley of the River Ayr. 14th June 1963, shows a Standard 5 No. 73006 passing Brackenhill box with a North-bound goods from Carlisle, while Crab No. 2805 waits to follow to Mauchline with the daily goods from Catrine to Ayr shortly before this service was withdrawn and the branch closed for good.

W.J.V.A.

Above left: "Britannia" 4–6–2 No. 70006 climbing the bank near Bowhouse, south of Kilmarnock, with a parcels and postal train, September 1964.

D.C.

Above: 26th May 1964, at Polquhap Summit on the Nith Valley Line, with one of Hurlford's "Crabs" starting the long descent across the Ayrshire Plateau with the morning coal train from Knockshinnoch Colliery (New Cumnock) to Hurlford Mineral Sidings. Loco No. 42879.   D.C.

Left: A fitted freight on the Nith Valley route between Thornhill and Closeburn leaves the hills behind as it heads south for Carlisle; Jubilee Class 4–6–0 No. 45687 "Neptune", May 1958.

W.J.V.A.

Below: The use of ten-coupled engines on the Nith Valley line reached its zenith in the early sixties, when one of the B.R. 9.F's was tested between Kilmarnock and Dumfries with the ex-LMS mobile testing unit. On this occasion one of the runs figured in the "Motor" magazine when some startled car tester was overtaken by the 9.F doing a stately 85–90 m.p.h. More prosaic, however, were the fairly regular appearances during the war and for some years after of the Austerity 2–10–0's on through freights between Carlisle and Glasgow. By the late fifties, however, these had become rare, and this photo of No. 90768 in August 1958, with a North-bound goods near Kirkconnel must be among their last appearances on this route.   D.C.

Left: Maid of all work in Ayrshire, "Crab" No. 42913 at Crosshouse, west of Kilmarnock, with a feather-weight freight taking the line to Dalry. The line in the foreground went to Irvine and is now closed; the Dalry line is still in use and looks like becoming the main link between Glasgow and Kilmarnock and the south when the Joint line through Barrhill is closed in the near future.　　　D.C.

Right: The small station of Kilmaurs, some 2 miles north of Kilmarnock on the Caley/G. and S.W. Joint line from Barrhill to Kilmarnock, was best known as the place where the London expresses started to apply their brakes after the hectic descent from the summit between Lugton and Dunlop. It also boasted one of the largest creameries in Ayrshire that entailed a shunt from Kilmarnock most mornings. 8th June 1963, finds ex-Caley 0–6–0 No. 57572 shunting the sidings at Kilmaurs, while "Crab" No. 42739 passes on the main line with a goods from Kilmarnock to Lugton and the Admiralty sidings at Giffen on the Branch (now closed) from Lugton to Beith.　　　D.C.

Section 4 Stirling – Perth

Left: A2 No. 60532 approaches Blackford crossing with the 1.30 p.m. from Aberdeen on a rainy day in June 1966.   J. R. P. Hunt.

Below: Ex-Caledonian 2F 0–6–0 No. 57460 poses at Stirling sheds.
    J. A. N. Emslie.

Right: B.R. Standard Caprotti Class 5 4–6–0 No. 73150 climbs Kinbuck Bank, north of Dunblane, with the 6.15 p.m. Glasgow, Buchanan Street to Dundee train, 26th August 1965. B. Stephenson.

Below: Class A4 Pacific No. 60016 "Silver King" heads the Southbound Postal near Gleneagles in Perthshire. May 1964.   W.J.V.A.

Left: In 1962 some of the Stanier Princess Royal Pacifics made a welcome come-back to service on the Perth to Carlisle route. No. 46201 "Princess Elizabeth" is here seen passing Whitemoss crossing not long after leaving Perth with the 4.45 p.m. fish and meat train on a Sunday in August. W.J.V.A.

Right: V2 2–6–2 No. 60919 at Hilton Junction with the "up" Postal. S. C. Crook.

Far right: The 9.30 a.m. Aberdeen to Glasgow train with A2 Pacific No. 60525 "A. H. Peppercorn" makes a spirited restart from the Perth stop in April 1961. W.J.V.A.

Left: The working of the tightly timed three-hour expresses between Glasgow and Aberdeen ensured that the Gresley Pacifics went out with a glorious swan-song. A3 No. 60090 "Grand Parade" heads the 5.30 p.m. from Aberdeen in place of the more usual A4. Circa 1963.
This train was some five minutes late, but there is obviously no shortage of steam here as she passes Hilton Junction, and from the way she was being driven it was probable that the new crew, who had just come on at Perth, would have the arrears made up on arrival at Stirling. W.J.V.A.

Left: One of the most beautiful products of Scottish engineering, ex-Caledonian 4–2–2 No. 123, thoughtfully restored to original condition, works a return excursion from Dundee to Glasgow near Auchterrarder in Perthshire in May 1958. Note the thistles etched into the buffers. W.J.V.A.

Right: A September 1959 excursion from Aberdeen to Glasgow climbs up through the Cumbernauld Glen behind ex-G.N.S.R. 4–4–0 No. 49 "Gordon High-lander" and ex-G.W.R. 4–4–0 "City-of-Truro", both restored to original condition. W.J.V.A.

Above: Jubilee Class 4–6–0 No. 45716 "Swiftsure" passes Hilton Junction with the 4.45 p.m. fish and parcels from Perth to the South. W.J.V.A.

Above right: B.R. Standard Class 5 No. 73009 approaches Dunblane on the 5.30 p.m. Glasgow to Aberdeen train "The Saint Mungo", April 1958, before the train was accelerated to do the journey in three hours. W.J.V.A.

Left: Shadows lengthen on an August evening in 1961 as Stanier Pacific No. 46241 "City of Edinburgh" passes Hilton Junction, just south of Perth, on the 8.15 p.m. to London. W.J.V.A.

Right: The Stanier 2–8–0's were common enough south of the border, but for some reason they rarely ventured North of the Solway. In 1963 the parcels traffic between Perth and Carlisle was normally handled by Stanier Pacifics, but for a few weeks in July the Pacifics must have been otherwise employed standing in for failed diesels. As a result, Stanier 2–8–0's made a few rare appearances at Perth. The parcels trains were not easily timed and doubtless some late arrivals were recorded; in any case, the Pacifics were soon back. In this picture No. 48464 passes Auchterrarder on the 12.30 p.m. parcels from Perth to Carlisle. W.J.V.A.

Left: For some reason the authorities at Doncaster cannot have been convinced of the advantages of double chimneys. Some of the later members of Class A2 emerged with single chimneys; surely a retrograde step. One of these, No. 60525 "A. H. Peppercorn", takes the Glasgow road at Hilton Junction with the 9.30 a.m. from Aberdeen. May 1960.   W.J.V.A.

Right: The 12.15 p.m. train from Perth to London, with Pacific No. 72009 "Clan Stewart", passes Hilton Junction just south of Perth. The other line goes to Edinburgh, via Glenfarg. September 1961.   W.J.V.A.

Left: Ex-Caledonian 0–6–0 No. 57576 leaves Stirling with a train for Callander. J. A. N. Emslie.

Right: One of the very last jobs to be performed by Caledonian 0–6–0's was the Stirling to Gleneagles pick-up goods. The reason for this was probably because one of the duties of this train was to work the branch to Gleneagles Hotel. In November 1960, No. 57572 in ex-works condition is still steaming hard as she runs downhill through Kinbuck on the return to Stirling. The shed plate on the smokebox door is 67B, which belongs to Hurlford near Kilmarnock.
W.J.V.A.

Far right: Gleneagles Station in September 1965; a few empty wagons stand at the platform where the Crieff branch train would have been waiting. On the main line, Pacific No. 72008 ''Clan Macleod'' restarts the 9.25 a.m. train from Crewe to Perth.
W.J.V.A.

Left: B.R. Standard 2–6–4T No. 80125 pulls the 12.5 p.m. train from Crieff to Gleneagles Junction between Muthil and Tullibardine. Several attempts were made to introduce diesel railcars and railbuses on this line, but the steep grades seemed to be too much for them; steam reigned supreme in the last years before closure.
W.J.V.A.

Below: Standard Pacific No. 72006 ''Clan Mackenzie'' runs downhill past Whitemoss crossing, near Auchterarder, on the 9.50 a.m. London to Perth train in September 1959. On the hill in the background – ''Craig Rossie'' – the Romans had an important outpost for keeping an eye on Strathearn.   W.J.V.A.

Right: Working the 9.25 a.m. Crewe to Perth, Stanier Class 5 No. 44899 coasts with steam shut off for the next stop at Gleneagles Station. May 1961.   W.J.V.A.

Section 5
Callander and Oban, Killin and Ballachulish Branches

Dunblane–Killin Junction

Left: A return excursion for Glasgow leaves Callander at dusk in October 1964. Ex-C.R. 4–2–2 No. 123   W.J.V.A.

Right: The 4.5 p.m. train from Callander to Killin for school-children only, climbs up Glenogle in June 1951; ex-Caledonian 0–4–4T No. 55263. This was a most spectacular stretch of track, but a headache to the Railway authorities who had to patrol it before every train to watch for fallen rocks. It was a rock slide near this spot that caused prema-ture closure.   W.J.V.A.

Left: March 1950, but not much sign of spring, with fresh snow low on the slopes of Ben More. Stanier Class 5 No. 45480 restarts the 12.5 p.m. Oban to Glasgow train out of Killin Junction Station. The branch to Killin is seen in front of the locomotive's buffer beam. W.J.V.A.

Below: The 12.5 p.m. Oban to Glasgow train approaches Glenoglehead hauled by Stanier Class 5 No. 45178 in March 1956. W.J.V.A.

Right: In April 1959, Class 5 No. 45460 climbs Glenogle on the 12.0 noon Glasgow to Oban train. The twist in the middle of the train as it changes super-elevations is most noticeable. W.J.V.A.

Below left: Stanier Class 5 No. 45460 restarts the 12.0 noon train from Glasgow (Buchanan Street) to Oban out of Loch Awe Station. In years gone by there was much interchange with steamboats plying Loch Awe at this point. Just in front of the exhaust steam the magnificent ruins of Kilchourn Castle can be seen.

Below right: Not long after, the same train is now following the spectacular "Pass of Brander". At this point the line is protected from falling rocks by an automatic signalling system. Something striking the stout wire fence above the railway causes signals to go to danger; one of these can be seen in the background. W.J.V.A.

Right: Class 4F 0–6–0 No. 44318, of Midland Railway design but built during the early years of the L.M.S., moves westwards out of Crianlarich with a freight for Oban. It was not common to see one of these engines on the Callander and Oban line. This one finally stalled just a few yards short of Tyndrum Lower Station. The mountain in the background is Ben More. W.J.V.A.

Left: One spring morning, early in the 1960s, the 7.50 a.m. Glasgow to Oban train became derailed while negotiating Glen Lochy crossing loop. Nobody was hurt. When this picture was taken, everything was back on the rails, the crane is about to return to Perth, and the suspect coaches continue to Oban very cautiously. W.J.V.A.

Right top: Easter weekend of 1963 must have boasted more extremes of weather over the southern half of Scotland than any weekend in April for many years. Good Friday dawned clear and cold, and the Caley single No. 123 set off from Glasgow on a round trip to Callander and Crianlarich via the Oban line, returning to Glasgow over the West Highland. As the train tackled the climb to Glen Ogle a short snow storm of great fury broke, and by the time the train got to Killin Junction the countryside was white. This photo, taken half a mile west of Luib Station, shows No. 123 and the two preserved Caledonian coaches running through the fresh snow, and has a timeless quality about it that makes it a photo that could have been taken half a century ago. D.C.

Right: Restored G.N.S.R. 4–4–0 "Gordon Highlander" approaches Glencruiten summit crossing shortly after leaving Oban with a return excursion to Glasgow. W.J.V.A.

The Killin Branch

Left: Killin Station, with the connecting bus to Aberfeldy. Branch train headed by 2–6–4T No. 80126. July 1965.   I. S. Krause.

Right: It is very rare to find a mixed train in Great Britain. In November 1963, B.R. Standard Tank No. 80126 works the 1.42 p.m. Killin to Killin Junction as a mixed train.   W.J.V.A.

Below: The 6.25 p.m. Killin to Killin Junction train near Lix Toll in August 1959. Ex-Caledonian Jumbo 0–6–0 No. 57246.   W.J.V.A.

Left: Ex-Caledonian 0–4–4T No. 55204 makes gentle, if somewhat smoky, progress not long after leaving Killin on the 6.55 p.m. to Killin Junction in May 1961.   W.J.V.A.

Right: Storm clouds over Killin, with 80126 bound for Killin Junction. July 1965.
          J. R. P. Hunt.

The Ballachulish Line

Right: Towards the end of the 1950s, the traffic in refined Bauxite to Ballachulish for the aluminium works at Kinlochleven increased to such an extent that it got beyond the powers of the old Caledonian Jumbo 0–6–0's that had worked the goods traffic on the branch from Connel Ferry since opening day. More powerful replacement came in the shape of No. 57667, a more modern Caledonian 0–6–0 of a class introduced in 1918 by Pickersgill. In this picture the newcomer heads the morning goods from Ballachulish to Connel along the shores of Loch Linnhie, near Kentallen. April 1958.   W.J.V.A.

Left: The 3.52 p.m. train from Ballachulish to Oban crosses the Connel Cantilever bridge over the Falls of Lora in March 1958. Ex-C.R. 0–4–4T No. 55263.
W.J.V.A.

Right: At 3.48 p.m., Caledonian 0–4–4T No. 55263 leaves Ballachulish with a train for Oban. May 1959.   W.J.V.A.

Perth

Left: Rebuilt "Scot" 4–6–0 No. 46162 "Queens Westminster Rifleman" catches the last rays of the setting sun as she pulls out of Perth with the 8.15 p.m. for London in April 1964. Standard 2–6–4T No. 80093 on shunting duty, discreetly hides the fact that the "Scot" is only pulling one van and one coach.
W.J.V.A.

Right: For two or three years A2 Pacific No. 60532 "Blue Peter" was standby engine at Dundee. She was not often to be seen at work. There was, however, one regular turn to keep her in trim, the 10.30 a.m. Sunday train to Glasgow and return. In this picture she is accelerating this train out of Perth in February 1962.
W.J.V.A.

Opposite: Fresh from Darlington Works, V2 2–6–2 No. 60955 about to leave Perth with an Edinburgh train. July 1965.

J. R. P. Hunt.

Left: Class V2 2–6–2 No. 60970 has brought the 1.50 p.m. fish train from Aberdeen into Perth Station and is shunting some wagons off the train. Britannia Pacific No. 70009 "Alfred the Great" waits to take the train over and depart for the south at 4.45 p.m. W.J.V.A.

Far left: Under the critical eye of a driver walking down the track-side to Friarton Depot, Standard Pacific No. 72008 ''Clan Macleod'' leaves Perth for the south on a fish train at 4.45 p.m. one afternoon in April 1965.
W.J.V.A.

Left: Perth was a very busy place early on a summer morning. The old lay-out was interesting in that both sides of the Station seemed to be used for both up and down trains. Here an up train, the 6.45 a.m. to Ladybank, pulls out of the main down platform behind an ex-Caledonian Jumbo 0–6–0 No. 57345. August 1950.
W.J.V.A.

Right top: In 1895, McIntosh introduced a powerful class of 0–6–0 tanks on the Caledonian railway. In 1957 one of them, No. 56331, shunts in Balhousie yard at the north end of Perth.
W.J.V.A.

Right centre: Jubilee Class 4–6–0 No. 45729 ''Furious'' accelerates the 5.30 p.m. Glasgow to Aberdeen express past Balhousie signal box in the outskirts of Perth. Shunting in the yard is ex-N.B.R. 4–4–0 No. 62484 ''Glen Lyon''. July 1958. W.J.V.A.

Right below: V2 2–6–2 No. 60819 pulls out of Perth with the 5.30 p.m. Glasgow to Aberdeen. July 1959.
W.J.V.A.

Right: 11.20 a.m. the clock says on a July morning in 1958. The bi-weekly goods train leaves Bankfoot, terminus of a light railway which left the main line at Strath Ord, just north of Perth. There seem to be some unauthorised additions to the crew making the 100 yard journey to the first level crossing. Ex-C.R. Jumbo 0–6–0 No. 57243.
W.J.V.A.

Left: Standard Class 5 No. 73005 on the 6.47 a.m. Perth – Inverness. August 1950.   W.J.V.A.

Right: A very important wagon of coal is hustled northwards out of Perth by ex-C.R. Jumbo 0–6–0 No. 57441. The River Tay can be seen through the trees.
W.J.V.A.

The Aberfeldy Branch

Right: The track on the Aberfeldy branch was in remarkably good condition so the drivers were not given to wasting time on the trip. In this February 1958 picture, ex-Caledonian 0–4–4T No. 55217 approaches Aberfeldy with the 1.8 p.m. from Ballinluig. W.J.V.A.

Below left: On a frosty afternoon in January 1958 a Caledonian 0–4–4T and one coach head back towards Ballinluig, the 1.55 p.m. from Aberfeldy. The snow-clad mountain in the background is Ben Lawers. W.J.V.A.

Below: The 4.38 p.m. Ballinluig to Aberfeldy train leaving Grandtully Station in November 1957. The engine is ex-CR 0–4–4T No. 55209. W.J.V.A.

Perth – Dunkeld – Dalnaspidal

Left: For many years Pickersgill 4–4–0's worked the "locals" between Perth and Blair Atholl. Modernisation came first in the shape of Stanier 2–6–4T's; then diesel railcars. However, in the summer of 1960 there was a shortage of railcars, the 2–6–4T's returned, but for some reason they ran short too; so back came the 4–4–0's for a few glorious weeks. Pickersgill 4–4–0 No. 54485 climbs from Dunkeld to Kingswood crossing on the 5.25 p.m. from Blair Atholl to Perth in September 1960. W.J.V.A.

Right: A Perth – Inverness relief train receives a signal check as it approaches Killiecrankie behind Standard Class 5MT 4–6–0 No. 73007. 30th July 1960.

B. Stephenson.

Section 7
The Highland Main Line

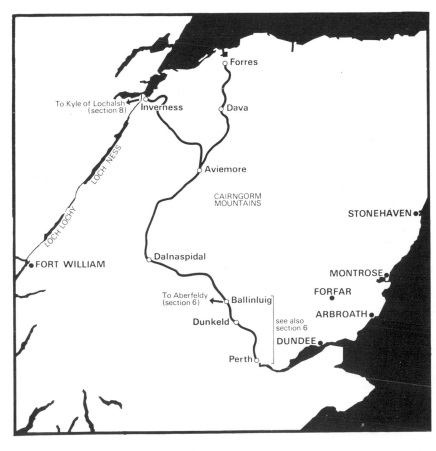

Below left: The 8.20 a.m. Inverness to Perth train near Rohallian, south of Dunkeld, in the spring of 1959. Stanier Class 5 No. 45488. W.J.V.A.

Below: In July 1960, Pickersgill 4–4–0 No. 54486 climbs from Dunkeld to Kingswood on the pick-up goods from Blair Atholl to Perth. W.J.V.A.

Below right: On a frosty November morning, the daily Blair Atholl to Perth pick-up goods passes Inchmagranachan, near Dunkeld, behind ex-Caledonian Pickersgill 4–4–0 No. 54486. November 1959. W.J.V.A.

Left: Very much on home territory, the restored Highland 4–6–0 No. 103 works an excursion south over the main line from Inverness to Perth. Dalnaspidal Station is only a few miles from the summit at Druimuachdar.
W.J.V.A.

Right: The Scottish Region of B.R. must be given credit for a stroke of genius in the Publicity field with the working of four pre-Grouping engines on excursions throughout the latter part of the 1950s and the first half of the 1960s. Of the engines preserved, the most interesting historically was the Jones Goods 4–6–0, ex-Highland Railway No. 103. The centenary of the Highland line in 1965, occasioned 103's return to her native heath for a week of exhibition runs between Inverness and Elgin. This photo, taken on the 30th August 1965, shows No. 103 returning south over the Highland main line passing the high and lonely station of Dalnaspidal, with a train composed of the two preserved Caledonian coaches.
D.C.

Dalnaspidal – Inverness
(and old H.R. Line)

Left: The 2.5 p.m. Inverness to Perth via Forres passes Allanfearn on the shores of the Beauly Firth with a Stanier Class 5 4–6–0 No. 45018 in January 1951. W.J.V.A.

Below: Druimuachdar Summit in the early afternoon of the 3rd January 1953. The sun shines with Alpine brilliance out of a cloudless sky, but it is cold and very still. The road is blocked and silence is complete. You first hear them when they are still some five miles away; then the sound ebbs and flows as it echoes amongst the hills, but it is always coming nearer, and finally builds up to a magnificent crescendo as they thunder past. They shut off steam for the descent into the Spey valley. Gradually silence returns as the wheels recede. Two Stanier Class 5's head the 11.55 a.m. Perth to Inverness train. W.J.V.A.

Right: A fully fitted train, twenty wagons of locomotive coal for Inverness depot, rolls to a stop at Slochd Summit box. The Pickersgill 4–4–0 No. 54482 will be uncoupled and will return to Aviemore. For the Stanier Class 5 No. 44924 it is downhill all the way to Inverness. July 1959. W.J.V.A.

Left: Standard Class 5 No. 73007 with the 2.5 p.m. train from Inverness to Perth on the long climb from Forres to Dunphail on the old Highland main line. February 1952. W.J.V.A.

Right: For some years Caledonian 4–4–0's were used for piloting from Aviemore to Slochd Summit. Around 1955 a Stanier 2–6–4T appeared on the job, a big improvement from the point of view of a crew making the tender first return to Aviemore on a snowy winter's night. The 2–6–4T was not always serviceable; her boiler had to be washed out, and on this happy occasion in the summer of 1959 she spent two months at St. Rollox under repair. In this August 1959 picture, Pickersgill 4–4–0 No. 54484 is piloting Stanier Class 5 No. 45473 on the 11.51 a.m. Perth to Inverness train about two miles north of Carrbridge in the defile of the Baddengorm burn. W.J.V.A.

Left: One of the belated effects of nationalisation was the closure of the yard at Boat-of-Garten and the extension of the Speyside goods to Aviemore. In this September 1960 picture, an ex-Caledonian 0–6–0 No. 57634 heads east out of Aviemore with the Speyside goods. The passenger coach near the rear of the train suggests it was a Monday morning, as there was an unbalanced Craigellachie to Aviemore train on a Saturday night known as the "Boozer". W.J.V.A.

Right: Caledonian Pickersgill 4–4–0's Nos. 54485 and 54486 move out of Kingussie on the North-bound Highland mail in April 1960. W.J.V.A.

Below: About a mile north of Aviemore two unidentified Stanier Class 5 4–6–0's haul the 12.5 p.m. Perth to Inverness via Carrbridge. The snow lies thick on the top of the Cairngorms, and the ice in the foreground looks good for skating. February 1960. W.J.V.A.

Left: The unsynchronised beats of two Stanier Class 5's was a familiar sound for many years along the route of the Highland Railway. No. 45452 and an unidentified sister aim south with the 3.40 p.m. Sunday train from Inverness to Perth in August 1957. They are tackling the long climb from Newtonmore to Dalwhinnie, and are getting into stride again after a slight easement through Etteridge crossing loop to change the tablet. Many things about this train are typical of the period; both engines with light smoke clouds and white feathers showing at their safety valves. If you look through the front cab window of the pilot engine you can see the section tablet hanging on a bracket on the front of the tender. In this case, the section concerned is Etteridge – Inchlea. The train itself consists of some fourteen vehicles; the Edinburgh coaches are in front of the restaurant car. The largest part of the train will go to Glasgow after reformation at Perth.   W.J.V.A.

Right: Just a few miles south of Inverness on the new main line to Perth is Culloden Moor Viaduct, one of the most expensive engineering features on the Highland Railway. In this May 1951 picture, a genuine Superheated Dunalastair IV, No. 54445 hauls a P.W. train from Inverness to Daviot. W.J.V.A.

Left: On a snowy day in December 1958, Stanier 2–6–4T No. 42269 pilots an unidentified Stanier Class 5 past Slochd Summit distant signal with a down goods. W.J.V.A.

Right: February 1951 was particularly difficult for Scottish Railways; the West Highland was snow blocked for days. The Highland managed to stay open. A journey north on the 6.47 a.m. ex-Perth to Inverness on the Monday morning after a particularly bad weekend was a memorable occasion Over the summit it was more like being in a ship on an endless sea of snow. Three engines were used to haul the train, and the noise from the wheels was completely deadened by snow.
There was not much snow at Aviemore, and the snow plough engine was there to photograph if it could be moved forward a wee bit. To the chagrin of the photographer, it was a bowler-hatted inspector who put his head out of the cabside in answer to a hail; but he proved most obliging. W.J.V.A.

Left: Two Caledonian Pickersgill 4–4–0's leave Aviemore with the North-bound mail from Perth to Inverness via Carrbridge in May 1960. The second vehicle is the ex-Highland mail van. W.J.V.A.

Section 8
The Farther North
and Kyle Lines

Inverness

Below left: Class 5 No. 44785 poses in front of the old Highland Railway water tower arch, Inverness sheds.   J. A. N. Emslie.

Right: Inverness Shed in October 1951. Ex-Caledonian 0–4–0 ST No. 56038, which was used to shunt the docks, and ex-Highland 0–4–4T No. 55051, one of the Dornoch branch engines.   W.J.V.A.

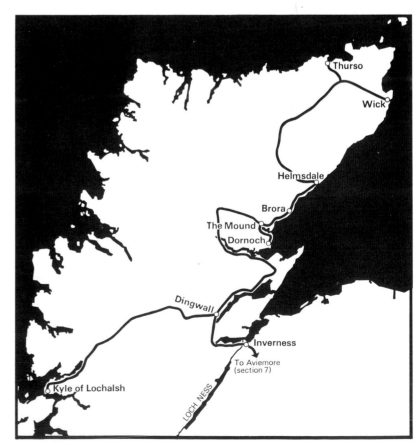

Left: Pickersgill C.R. 4–4–0 No. 54470 at Inverness with the 3.14 p.m. train to Tain. 14th September 1959.   B. Stephenson.

Below left: One of the first batch of Pickersgill Superheated 4–4–0's with the 3 p.m. Inverness to Tain local crossing the swing bridge over the Caledonian Canal at Clachnaharry. The Beauly Firth and part of the Black Isle can be seen behind. May 1951.   W.J.V.A.

Below right: Ex-H.R. Clan Goods No. 57956 hauls the 3 p.m. train for Tain in the outskirts of Inverness. The engine is equipped with a small snow plough. In spite of the fact this was November 1952 the tender is still painted L.M.S. The second coach is a twelve-wheeled Caledonian one.   W.J.V.A.

The Kyle Line

Below: The last regular passenger steam turns on the Highland were the mail trains to Kyle. In this picture Stanier Class 5 No. 45117 crosses the River Bran, shortly after leaving Achanalt on the East-bound mail 10.45 a.m. ex-Kyle of Lochalsh. May 1962.

W.J.V.A.

Right: Stanier Class 5 4–6–0 No. 45473 climbs the steep grade just west of Loch Luichart Station; the train is the 10.40 a.m. mail from Inverness to Kyle of Lochalsh.

W.J.V.A.

Below: Ex-Highland Railway Jones Goods 4–6–0 No. 103 in restored condition works the 5.40 p.m. Inverness to Kyle of Lochalsh train in May 1960. The train is stopping at Lentran Station on the shores of the Beauly Firth. The louvres at the front of the chimney were peculiar to certain of the older Highland engines. Their object was to deflect the smoke upwards during long spells of coasting downhill. W.J.V.A.

Right: Class 5 No. 44978, en route to Kyle of Lochalsh, pauses at Strome Ferry Station with the 1962 R.C.T.S./S.L.S. Rail Tour train. S. E. Teasdale.

Opposite right: Ex-Caledonian 0–4–4T No. 55227 outside the shed at Kyle of Lochalsh. 7th September 1961. B. Stephenson.

Below: In May 1960, the 5.40 p.m. stopping train from Inverness to Kyle of Lochalsh pulls out of Achnasheen Station. This desolate spot was approximately half way between Kyle and Dingwall. In olden days trains stopped here long enough for passengers to reinforce themselves in the adjoining hotel. The locomotive is the first 4–6–0 to run in Great Britain; it was constructed in 1894 for the Highland railway.   W.J.V.A.

Right: The restored Jones Goods at Kyle of Lochalsh terminus in June 1961. As can be judged from the photograph, this is the sort of place where a cautious approach is recommended. A coasting vessel can be seen in Lochalsh behind. The hills on the other side are part of the Isle of Skye; the prominent peak is Ben Na Caillich.   W.J.V.A.

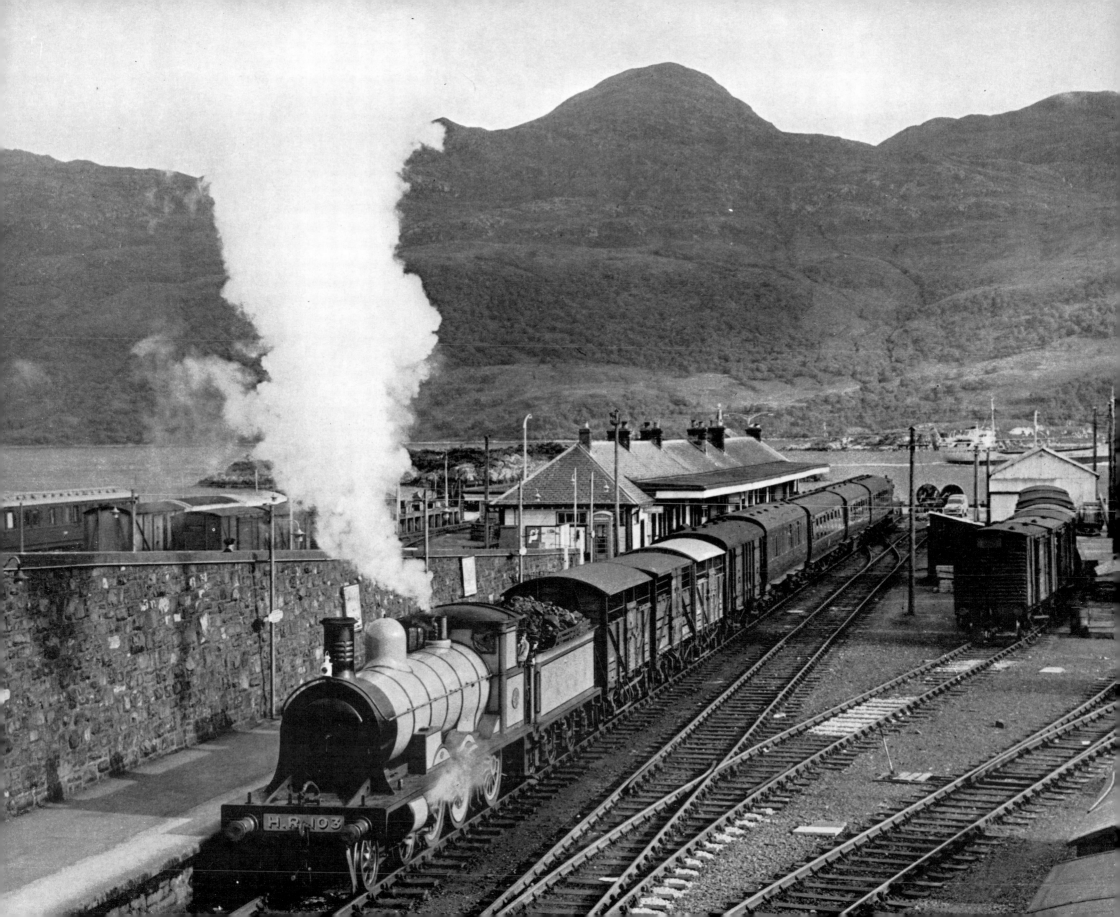

The Dornoch Branch

Left: W.R. 16XX Class 0–6–0 PT No. 1646 waits at Cambusavie with the 11.55 a.m. Mound to Dornoch mixed train as the guard walks forward to open the crossing gates. 10th September 1959.

B. Stephenson.

Below: The same engine at Dornoch, with the 1.00 p.m. train to the Mound. 10th September 1959.

B. Stephenson.

Below right: 1646 shunts the 11.55 a.m. mixed train for Dornoch at the Mound before departing for Dornoch. 10th September 1959.

B. Stephenson.

Left: In October 1956, the 10.40 a.m. mixed train from Dornoch to the Mound crosses Loch Fleet on a causeway built for the road, long before the coming of the railway, by the famous engineer Telford. The engine is one of Peter Drummond's delightful little 0–4–4T's built for branch line service on the Highland Railway in 1905.

The year 1956 marked the centenary of the Inverness and Aberdeen Junction Railway, the first constituent of the Highland Railway. By this time 55053 was the only active Highland engine, and the Scottish Region management had the happy idea of giving her a thorough overhaul and repaint fully lined-out in North Western colours.

W.J.V.A.

Below: The 2.5 p.m. train from the Mound to Dornoch, near Skelbo, in October 1959; ex-Highland 0–4–4T No. 55053. W.J.V.A.

Left: Ex-Caledonian 4–4–0 No. 54496 poses in Wick Station. 11th September 1959.   B. Stephenson.

Right: The same engine pauses during shunting operations at Wick. 11th September 1959.   B. Stephenson.

Below: Class 5 4–6–0 No. 45496 takes water at Helmsdale before detaching the T.P.O. and Restaurant Car from the 11.05 Inverness to Wick train. The T.P.O. is a former Highland Railway vehicle. 8th September 1959.   B. Stephenson.

Below left: Class 5 4–6–0 No. 44997 approaches Brora with an Inverness to Wick freight. 8th September 1959. B.Stephenson.

Below right: The 8.35 a.m. from Wick to Inverness runs through Strath Fleet behind Stanier Class 5 No. 45123. The next station is Rogart, one of the 39 stops (steps) on this long but beautiful journey. October 1956. W.J.V.A.

Below left: Class 5 4–6–0 No. 45098 waiting in the passing loop at Brora with a Wick to Inverness freight for the 11.25 Inverness to Wick (Mail) train to pass. 8th September 1959.
B. Stephenson.

Below right: Class 5 4–6–0 No. 44784 climbs slowly but surely up the steep grade from Invershin to Lairg in the far north of Scotland. A good part of the considerable load is empty cattle wagons bound for Lairg and the Lairg Sales. Even in a remote spot like this, there is a plethora of electric wires about. W.J.V.A.

Top left: Class 5 4–6–0 No. 45117 shunting at Helmsdale. 8th September 1959.
B. Stephenson

Bottom left: Automatic token exchange taking place at Brora, as Class 5 4–6–0 No. 44998 hurries through with an Inverness to Wick fitted freight. 1st August 1960.
B. Stephenson.

Right: Freight leaving Alness for Inverness behind Pickersgill 0–6–0 No. 57661, September 1959.
S. C. Crook.